Moffat . . . A Backward Glance.

Sheila Forman

with revisions by Neil Wilson

LOCHAR PUBLISHING · MOFFAT · SCOTLAND

British Library Cataloguing in Publication Data

Moffat. – : a backward glance. - 2nd ed.
1. Moffat (Dumfriesshire) - History
I. Title II. Wilson, Neil, *1955 -*
941.4'83   DA890.M75

ISBN 0-948403-04-7

First published c. 1949
©Lochar Publishing 1987
Bankhead
Annan Water
MOFFAT DG10 9LS
Tel: 0683 - 20916

Designed by Lochar Publishing
Typeset by Dumfries ITeC
Printed by Kelvinprint Ltd, Cumbernauld

ACKNOWLEDGEMENTS

Lochar Publishing gratefully acknowledges the support of
Mrs Kathy Bacon and the family of the late Sheila
Forman. The publishers would also like to thank those
people in Moffat who selflessly contributed to this
publication, in particular Mrs Jean Cockayne, Terence
Leigh, George Hood, Mr&Mrs T. Martin, also Mrs Karen
Cunningham of The Queen Mother Library, University
of Aberdeen and The Scots Magazine which first
published some of the material in June 1949. Special
thanks to Allan Wright and Jim McEwan for preparing
prints and photographs.

PICTURE CREDITS

Front cover: Neil Wilson.
Pages 2,11 : Maps courtesy of Ewart Library, Dumfries.
Pages 3,6,7,10,14,15,18,19,22,27: The George
Washington Wilson Photographic Collection, University
of Aberdeen.
Pages 23,26 : Mrs Jean Cockayne.
Rear Cover : Allan Wright Photography.

Merlin, Monks and Murderers

From the Edinburgh Road where it overlooks the cavernous bowl of the Devil's Beef Tub, stretches southward one of the most superb views in the Lowlands. Near the head of the green, wooded valley which emerges from the sombre heights enclosing the Tub, lies Moffat 'the little capital of Upper Annandale.' The word 'Annan' derived from the Gaelic term for 'slow running water' and Moffat, also said to originate from the Celtic 'Magh ubh at' (pronounced Moo-uv-at), meaning a deep mountain hollow, are self-descriptive.

Moffat is perhaps better known than any town of its size in Dumfriesshire, not only in Scotland but also far over the Border. Geographically it is well placed, being at the crossroads of the Carlisle – Glasgow dual carriageway (A74) and the Edinburgh – Dumfries route (A701). Its fame as a Spa still lives although Medicine today is less confident of the miraculous powers of the mineral waters which in other centuries were prescribed for all manner of ills. Set in grand natural surroundings, the town is a good centre for walking, climbing, sporting and for longer expeditions into more remote country. Above all, Moffat is memorable for a quality too restful to be called charm which, undisturbed by the bustle of the outside world, lies perhaps in the deep-rooted peace and stillness of the surrounding hills.

After the Roman occupation of what is now called Dumfriesshire, roughly between AD 80 and AD 446 , Britons, Picts, Danes and Norse invaders struggled for a foothold in the land. Amongst the Britons, the pagan Celtic tribe of the Selgovae predominated in Annandale and it was to their heartland that the seer Merlin fled after the Battle of Arderydd (Arthuret) in AD 573. Grieved by the slaying of his Lord Gwenddolau, he went mad and spent the remaining years of his life on the slopes of Hartfell.

At the very centre of the ancient Caledon Forest, the mountain - clearly seen from the A701 on the brim of the Beef Tub - was of great mystical significance to the Selgovae, for it was not only the watershed of the rivers Annan, Clyde and Tweed, but also the source of a sacred Chalybeate spring. This was described by the historian Geoffrey of Monmouth in his *Vita Merlini* published around 1150 as being 'on the very top of a certain mountain, surrounded on all sides by hazels and dense thorns. Merlin had settled there, and from that place he could watch the whole woodland'. In this most remote lair, befriended only by the forest animals, he uttered the prophecies which were to influence generations throughout mediaeval Britain and beyond. But there is no documentary evidence of a community living on the site of the present-day Moffat until about the Norman

Gallow Hill
Sur 852.0
Kings Chair
Hydropathic Establishment
Charlies Hope
Holmfield
Willow Bank
Ellerslie
Sunnybank
Woodside
Coldwell
Woodbine
Abington Villa
Balmorino
Elvan Villa
Hollin Bank
Springbank
Bankdale
Gilbert House
Annanlea
Laurel Bank
Lilly Bank
Westvale
Ravannah
Charlesville
Bowling Green
New Bridge
Croquet Green
The Whins
Academy
Larchhill
Grounds
Larchhill House
Nursery
Hepburn Place
Moffat
Moffat House
Pleasure
Bath Rooms
Park
Ashfield Lodge
Beechwood
Plantation foot
Gallows Well
Glendyne
Hartfell House
Greenwood Hall
Gallow House
Douglas Villa
Lyne Bank
Mayfield
Binhill
Marlfield
Rosegate Cottage
Martfield
Church
Manse
Lady Knowe
Episcopal Chapel
Police Station
Industrial School
Free Church
The Glebe
Old Bridge
The Kerr
The Crooks Meadows
The Crooks
Old Gill
Well head
Mill Dam
Arnibank
Foot Bridge
Site of Fort
Bearmead Knowe
Oldmill
Sparrow Hill
Mill Dam
Heatheryhaugh
Auldton
Old Well Road
Well Road
Church Road
Site of Fort
Burnock Lodge
Huntly Lodge
Penrose Hill
North Park
Woodlands
Burnrock
Belmont
Episcopal
Tiffany Lodge
Rockbern Cottage
Marchfoot
Glassmount
Rosemount
Auldton Moat
Hope Lodge
Sidmount Cottage
Greenbank Cottage
Well
Silbank House
Burnside Cottage
Vearlands
Meg Tod's Mote
Meadow Cottage
Floral Cottage
Burnbraes
Milbank House
Mill Burn
Milburnfoot
Mill Dam
St Germans
Eastfield
Eller Bank
Wellview
Dunmore Villa
Ballplay Road
Warriston Lodge
Hamilton House
Willowton Cottage
Ostrey Cottage
Burnbank
Mansfield
Moffat Holm
Fairfield
Holmend
Quernsbery Villa
Ferm lea
Roseville
Elinsville
Milton Villa
Etrick Bank
Kelsick Lodge
Ardenholm
Windsor Cottage
Nursery
S.M.s
Gill Lodge
Reference

*The approach to Moffat from Beattock, c 1876, with the old St Andrew's Kirk (centre - left)
and the Industrial School on Milburn (extreme   right)*

Conquest. This small settlement, thought to be mainly Saxon, was then ensconced on the lower slopes of the Gallows Hill to the north of Moffat, and soon after became one of the five parishes of Upper Annandale.

The Gallows Hill had, of course, at one time its gallow tree out on the bare hillside where the community could see offenders swinging in the breeze to warn them of the consequences of breaking the law. At the time of Robert the Bruce, the Lordship of Annandale carried with it 'the privileges of forage and provisions for a large retinue; so many fat cows and geese; and the power to hang, drown, banish, cut off a man's ears, nail them to a post, or burn his house over a man's head'. Much of this power remained with Scottish lords well into mediaeval times and feudal jurisdiction was not legally abolished until 1747, although by that time the 'heritable rights' had been modified. "Ye'll get your heid in your hands and your lugs to play wi'!" was a common saying in Dumfriesshire which once held more than an empty threat. A condemned man knew that resistance often endangered his wife and family and there is a story of an Annandale thief waiting for the gallows to be made ready who was reproved by his wife for showing signs of restiveness. "Come up quietly and be hanged", she said severely, "and do not anger the laird".

As early as 1218 Robert the Bruce granted to a Roger Crispm, in return for 'homage and service' certain lands round Moffat, including that now known as Rogermoor which probably takes the name from this ancient proprietor. A century later bake-houses, brew-houses, maltkilns and 'Yill selling' (ale selling) are mentioned which shows that Moffat, like other hamlets or 'villas' of Dumfriesshire, carried on these activities as well as their agricultural pursuits. In fact at a later date a Johnstone of Corehead who was a Superior of Moffat at the time complains that 'the Tennants take no care of stock but of their brewing and Yill selling'. Labour was cheap in those days, the unskilled workman being paid one old penny a day while carpenters and craftsman might receive three old pence. But commodities were also cheap (in 1263 a cow was sold for 22p and a sheep for 4p) and the Moffat community thought themselves comfortably well off.

The monks were the great patrons of agriculture in these early days and their lands were better cultivated than those of the lay proprietors. Much of the land round Moffat was owned by the Knights Templar or Red Friars who had a settlement on a ridge to the west of the town where the ruined gables of their chapel are still to be seen adjoining Chapel Farm. A rich and influential Order which rose swiftly during Crusading times, they professed the defence of the Holy Temple and the entertainment of pilgrims. The Vatican, however, disapproved of their increasing power and in 1316 they were finally suppressed by Pope Clement V.

William Wallace, barely out of his teens, fought and won his first battle for Scottish freedom on the lower slopes of Queensberry in a ravine still called "The bledy Gill". His sister was married to the laird of Corehead Castle, standing at the entrance to the Devil's Beef Tub, then called the Corrie of Annan, and it was there he gathered a small band of supporters and rode off on the pretext of 'hearing Mass' at Lochmaben. He succeeded in wresting Lochmaben Castle from the English and was hailed as a great leader in the cause of Scottish liberty from that time.

Moffat was not far enough away from the English border to escape the constant raiding and marauding between the two countries during the 15th and 16th Centuries. When the enemy was sighted on the Border the alert was blazed through Annandale by a series of beacons. The first signal flared from Repentence watch-tower which overlooked the Solway and the Cumberland Hills, and from there the fiery message swept down the valley till it reached the last outpost on the Gallows Hill above Moffat. Families and goods were gathered within the stone walls of Peel Towers and the live-stock hurried into the basement. Those without a stone fortress often drove their cattle into the hills, sometimes as far as the Beef Tub and as high as Loch Skene, which as hiding-places were also useful deposits for plunder after an attacking foray.

The security of a stone tower, however, was desirable not only on account of the English. Divided loyalties and clan feuds were responsible for the ceaseless warfare which raged on well into the 17th Century in the Borders where fortifications were necessary long after they had become obsolete in more peaceful parts of the country. Of these strongholds round Moffat, which were both home and fortress, Loch House Tower is the only one which is still inhabited today without any radical alteration having been made to the structure. The tower stands a mile outside Moffat on the way to Beattock and was held by the superior Johnstone clan who also owned Raecleugh, Greskine and Blacklaw in the Evan valley, now all completely ruinous. To the east of Moffat stand the picturesque remains of Frenchland Tower, dating from about 1590, which was built by the French family who held lands in Moffat as early as the 12th Century. The Cornal Tower, now a crumbling pile of stones but once a stout fortress commanding the Moffat Water valley, was part of the Logan estate up to 1512 when it passed to the Carruthers and later became Douglas property.

The powerful Johnstone clan, which later dominated Annandale, were probably descended from Sir Gilbert de Johnston, one of the Norman immigrants, whose name is attached to the Bruce charters of the late 12th and early 13th Centuries. Unfortunately their early family records perished in the burning of Lochwood Castle by the Maxwells in 1585, so the exact date of their settlement in the district is not known. By that time, however, the head of the Lochwood family was chief laird of Upper Annandale which he remains today, the present representative being Mr Patrick Hope-Johnstone of Raehills. A contemporary account of the capture of Lochwood Castle vividly describes the methods of warfare employed at the times.

We came there about an hour before day; and the greater part of us lay close without the barmkin: But about a dozen of the men got over the barmkin wall, and stole close into the house within the barmkin, and

St Andrew's Kirk, c 1887, newly constructed with the buffers at the end of the railway to Beattock in the foreground

The Black Bull Hotel, c 1876, where Clavers was billeted two centuries before. The building which now serves as the Post Office had just been built at the top of the High Street

took the wenches and kept them secure in the house till daylight. And at sunrising, two men and a woman being in the tower, one of the men rising in his shirt, and going to the tower head, and seeing nothing stir about, he called on the wench that lay in the tower, and bade her rise and open the tower door and call up them that lay beneath. She so doing and opening the iron door, and a wood door without it, our men with (in) the barmkin brake a little too soon to the door; for the wench perceiving them, leapt back into the tower, and had gotten almost the wood door to, but one got hold of it that she could not get it close to so the skirmish rose, and we over the barmkin and broke open the wood door, and she being troubled with the wood door left the iron door open, and so we enterd and wan the Lochwood; where we found truly the house well purveyed for beef salted, malt, big (i.e. barley), hevermeal (i.e. oatmeal), butter and cheese.

In the 17th Century, the Johnstones received the titles of Earl of Hartfell and Annandale, Viscount of Annand, Lord Johnstone of Lochwood, Moffatdale and Evandale and in 1701, William III raised these to a marquisate. In 1792, on the death of the third Marquis, the titles became dormant and the property went to his grand-nephew, the Earl of Hopetoun. His daughter, Lady Anne Johnstone-Hope, inherited the Annandale estates while the Hopetoun property passed to the male line. Recently the titles returned to Patrick Hope-Johnstone after submissions to the House of Lords had been successfully received.

THE KIRK AND THE KILLING TIMES

The date of Moffat's first church is not known but in 1174 the existing one was transferred to the Bishopric of Glasgow. From this time up to the Reformation, it remained one of the prebends of Glasgow where the Rector lived 'in the Rottenrow, lapped in security and comfort, enjoying the luxury of repose' while a curate or vicar looked after his parish in Moffat. In early times the pastor combined with his spiritual duties, those of policeman and sheriff. Thus when one of the parishioners had been robbed, assaulted or otherwise injured, he went to the parson and 'took out letters of cursing' which amounted to the issuing of a warrant. After the Sabbath service, the intimations 'proclaimed in a loud voice' would be of this nature. "The wife at Braehead has tint a spurtle (lost a porridge stirrer). There is ane flail (a whip) stolen from the gudeman of the Howslack. The gudewife at Holmend has tint ane horn spoon. God's malison (evil one) and mine I give to them that know of this gear and restores it not".

One ruined wall of the pre-Reformation church still stands in the old cemetery but there are few really old tombstones for most of these were taken down in 1747 when the whole area was re-covered with four feet of new earth to make room for further burials. This fact detracts from the traditional belief that Protestants refused to be buried with Catholics and insisted on being raised to at least a slightly higher level of soil, for by 1747 Protestants had been gathered into the Kirkyard for over two hundred years. John Louden Macadam, of road-making fame, who died in Moffat in 1836, is buried here. He had connections with Moffat for his grandmother had married, as her second husband, Dr Robert Johnstone, 'Chirurgeon in Moffat', and during the years 1783-4 Macadam rented Dumcrieff House on the banks of the Moffat Water.

It was in this Kirkyard that Claverhouse ordered the inhabitants of Moffat to take the Test Oath in 1685 but that day many were absent behind drawn blinds and over the hillsides. Towards the end of the 18th Century, the old Kirk fell into a state of disrepair and one Sabbath, during the service, 'an alarm of impending fall arose and there was an instant crush towards the door.' The Reverend Alexander Brown, who was minister at the time, seems to have dealt wisely with the situation and no one was hurt. It was during his ministry that the precentor, deputising for him one Sabbath, proclaimed the banns of four couples, in the wrong order, first reading the names of the four men, followed by those of their intended brides. This caused a 'general imperilment of the decorum of the audience' but when the minister reproved him afterwards for the mistake, the precentor remained unperturbed. "Hoot toot, sir!" he said, "nae fear, nae fear, every yin will ken their ane".

The next parish Kirk, a simple unpretentious building, followed in 1790 and stood close to the site of the present St. Andrew's Church which was put up in the favourite neo-Gothic style of the time and celebrates its Centenary in 1987. The old barn-like Free Kirk was built in 1843, immediately after the Secession and the present St. Mary's, at the other end of the town, in 1892. The U.P. congregation, which existed early in the 18th Century, was not housed in the Well Road Church till 1862, the year in which it was built, but since demolished.

In 1610 Dr Whiteford, afterwards Bishop of Brechin, was appointed to the 'pastorate' of Moffat. An able and learned man, he was a strong upholder of Episcopacy, supporting the King and the Bishops against the growing resistance to ritual in Scotland. That he was well liked and trusted in Moffat probably accounts for the fact that while he was there, little opposition was made to the enforcement of Episcopal forms or the re-instatement of various practices thought by many to smack of Popery. Even in Brechin, whence he was called in 1630, he seems to have carried the people with him at first, although he was the last Bishop in Scotland to persist in reading Charles' Liturgy from the pulpit, to which he ascended in the latter days of his ministry with two loaded pistols. Eventually, however, he shared the fate of his brethren, being forced to flee to England 'the asylum of the scandalous Scotch Bishops.'

Later in the century, during the 'Killing Times,' Moffat was the centre of great Covenanting activities and hatred of Claverhouse (also known as "Bonnie Dundee" and "Bloody Clavers"), who was billeted at the Black Bull in 1678, smouldered for many years after his savageries had outraged the countryside. As recently as the end of the

Moffat High Street, c 1873, prior to the construction of the Post Office building and the Colvin Fountain

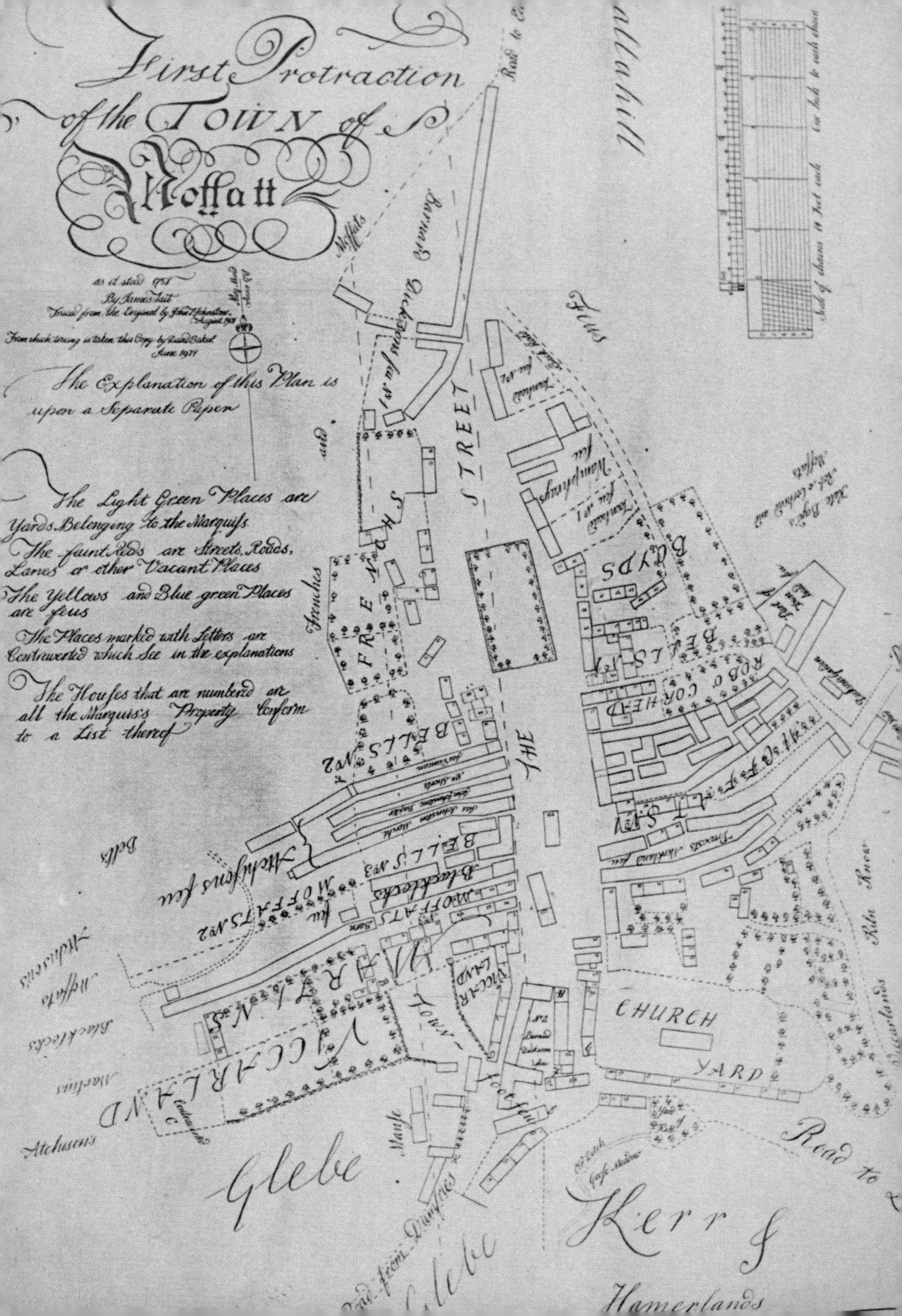
First Protraction of the Town of Moffatt
as it stood 1761
By James hait
Traced from the Original by John Johnstone August 1911
From which Drawing is taken this Copy by Rich.d Baker June 1971
The Explanation of this Plan is upon a Separate Paper
The Light Green Places are Yards Belonging to the Marquiss
The faint Reds are Streets, Roads, Lanes or other Vacant Places
The Yellows and Blue green Places are feus
The Places marked with Letters are Contrueeted which See in the explanations
The Houses that are numbered are all the Marquiss's Property Conform to a List thereof
Moffats
Barnard Dickson's Ground
STREET
Feus
allahill
Scale of chains 11 feet each
ten feet to each chain
FRENCHS
Frenches
THE
BELLS No 2
Atchisons feu
Bells
MOFFATS No 2
Blacklocks
BELLS No 3
Andersons feu
BUYDS
BELLS No 1
ROODO CORHEAD
FEUS
FEUS
TOWN
VICCAR LAND
VICCARLAND
YARDS No 5
Manse
GLEBE
Glebe
Road from Dumfries
CHURCH YARD
Kerr s
Hamerlands
Road to
Pitts River
Blacklocks
Martins
Moffats
Atchisons

last century, shepherds living in the hills and valleys between Moffat and Tweedsmuir would kill a whaup (a curlew) on sight, as their forefathers had done when the birds were dreaded informers of the Covenanters' hiding places. A body of Moffat adherents to the Covenant sheltered for many months in the fastnesses of Hartfell, 'terrified to expose themselves to still greater hardships, knowing full well that the eagle eye of Claverhouse would soon be upon them if they ventured to leave their seclusion.' John Hunter, shot dead by the dragoons and whose memorial stands opposite the hillside near Corehead where he fell, was not the only martyr to the cause.

Bodesbeck, up the solitary Moffat Water valley, sheltered Covenanters from all over the countryside. James Hogg, who knew every step of that wild region, describes vividly their strange mode of life in his novel *The Brownie of Bodsbeck.*

From the midst of that inhospitable wilderness, from those dark morasses, and unfrequented caverns - the prayers of the persecuted race nightly rose to the throne of the Almighty - prayers, as all testified who heard them, fraught with the most simple pathos, as well as bold and vehement sublimity. In the solemn gloom of the evening, after the last rays of day had disappeared, and again in the morning, before they began to streamer the east, the song of praise was sung to that Being, under whose fatherly chastisement they were patiently suffering. These psalms, always chaunted with ardour and wild melody, and borne on the light breezes of the twilight, were often heard at a great distance. The heart of the peasant grew chill, and his hairs stood all on end as he hasted home to alarm the cottage circle with a tale of horror. Lights were seen moving by night in wilds and caverns where human thing never resided, and where the foot of man seldom had trode.

The shepherds were certain, or believed they were certain, that no human being frequented these places; and they believed as well they might, that whole hordes of spirits had taken possession of their remote and solitary dells.

In November 1745 a company of Charles Edward's Highland army spent a night at Ericstane Braefoot and 'marched in good order into Moffat the next morning'. In fact the high standard of discipline at this stage of the march south seems to have left Moffat no incidents to record. Six Moffat men, however, who joined the rebels found a very unpleasant reception awaiting them when they returned two years later, for 'the inhabitants of the town rose against them and would have them killed, but the men having been trained by the rebels in the use of the broad sword, threatened if they were molested they would kill every man, woman and child in the place and burn all the houses.' The minister intervened and 'stayed the inhabitants from shedding blood', advising the men to leave the town 'which they did in the early morning, and they were seen going in the direction of Dumfries in company with six women natives of Moffat, known to everybody to be common randies'.

The Devil's Beef Tub

In 1747 another Moffat Jacobite, who was being marched to prison, escaped the guard of Cumberland soldiers by rolling down the steep side of the Beef Tub. Whether this was the man whom Sir Walter Scott met in his youth, and whose description of the incident he afterwards put into the mouth of the Laird of Summertrees in *Redgauntlet*, is not certain, but the experience must have been much the same.

Ye ken the place they call the Marquis's Beef-stand, because the Annandale loons used to put their stolen cattle in there? Ye must have seen it as ye came this way; it looks as if four hills were laying their heads together, to shut out daylight from the dark, hollow space between them. A deep, black, blackguard-looking abyss of a hole it is, and goes straight down from the roadside as perpendicular as it can do to be a heathery brae. At the bottom there is a small bit of a brook you would think could hardly find its way out from the hills that are so closely jammed round it...

Bad as the place was, Sir, it was my only chance; and though my very flesh creeped when I thought what a rumble I was going to get, yet I kept my heart up all the same. And so, just when we came on the edge of this beefstand of the Johnstones, I slipped out my hand from the handcuff . . . and whisked under the belly of the dragoon's horse - flung my plaid round me with the speed of lightning - threw myself on my side, for

there was no keeping my feet - and down the brae hurled I, over heather and fern, and blackberries, like a barrel down Chalmer's Close in Auld Reekie.

I never can help laughing when I think how the scoundrel red-coats must have been bombazed; for the mist being, as I said, thick, they had little notion, I take it, that they were on the edge of such a dilemma. I was halfway down - for rolling is faster work than running - ere they could get at their arms; and then it was flash, flash, flash - rap, rap, rap - from the edge of the road; but my head was too jumbled to think either of that or the hard knocks I got among the stones. I kept my senses thegither, whilk has been thought wonderful by all that ever saw the place, and I helped myself with my hands as gallantly as I could, and so to the bottom I came. There I lay for half a moment; but the thought of the gallows is worth all the salts and scent-bottles in the world for bringing a man to himself . . . . And so off I set, and never buck went faster over the braes than I did, and I never stopped till I had put three waters, reasonably deep, as the season was rainy, half a dozen mountains, and a few thousand acres of the worst moss and ling in Scotland, betwixt me and my friends the red-coats.

Today, the Beef Tub harbours no such hardship for the surefooted visitor, who can, on foul day or fair, take time to view as broad and captivating a landscape as is likely to be seen anywhere in the Lowlands of Scotland. A recently erected 'map-stone' on the brink of the rim by the A701 explains the view to passers-by.

Looking south towards the old Meal House by the Mercat Cross, c 1873

The same view, c 1876, after the Bank of Scotland and the Colvin Fountain had been built

TOWN AND TRADE

The Black Bull, which is one of the oldest houses in Moffat, was owned in the 18th Century by the Duncan family who in 1762 built the Annandale Arms (then the King's Arms). It is said that the masons employed there who were paid eight old pence a day, left the job to start work at Moffat House which was begun the same year, for a penny a day more. Moffat House, built for the Earl of Hopetoun, then in charge of the Annandale Estates, was designed by John Adam, one of the famous architect brothers. This delightful building, with its severe symmetry offset by the slightly curving roofs and facade connecting the wings to the main block, is Moffat's finest architectural possession and adds much to the present aspect of the High Street.

The old bowling-green, situated in the High Street and surrounded by a high Yew hedge, was renowned throughout the county and was often the scene of great social activity. It was patronised by a number of 18th century personalities including James Boswell, Dr Johnson's biographer; David Hume, the philosopher; John Home, the minister-playwright who scandalised the Presbytery, and James McPherson who is said to have written the first part of his 'Ossian's Poems' in Moffat. A contemporary history gives the following description of the High Street at this time. 'At the bowling green were to be seen sauntering, city clergy, men of letters, county gentlemen and ladies of rank and fashion; while the diseased, decrepit of the lowest rank, who had toilsomely travelled from far-off districts to taste the magic waters, loitered in their rags in the village street'.

Moffat had by now progressed a long way from the mediaeval hamlet clustered round the Gallows Hill with its bake-houses and brew-houses, its 'Yill' manufacture and Border forays. Since 1662, when the privilege of regality and the right of holding markets was conferred on the town, relationships with county had become closer and trade brisker. In 1790 Moffat counted 50 weavers, 6 shoemakers, 6 tailors, 8 merchants, 1 watchmaker, 2 bakers, 1 butcher, 1 barber, 5 masons, 6 wrights, 1 physician and 1 surgeon. The population was then about 1600 and even in those days housing was apparently a problem for the minister recorded ' There are no houses uninhabited. Some new ones were lately built and more are building at present; yet the inhabitants can hardly be accommodated.'

Good crops of potatoes were grown and turnip and clover were also successfully cultivated but 'the whole grain produced in the parish would not do more than supply the inns in the village.' The farmers evidently preserved a shrewd silence about their stocks even in those days for the minister continues 'the sheep farmers or storemasters are not much disposed to publish or make known the amount of their respective flocks; but it is supposed that there are in all from 18,000 to 20,000 sheep.' The prices of 'aged sheep' ran between £12 and £14 per score and for lambs £3.75 - £6.00. About 200 packs of wool were exported annually, mainly to England, and sold at about 20p per stone. New milk cost one old penny a pint and butter nine old pence a pound. A considerable number of goats were kept in the neighbourhood, the whey being in great demand by visitors who came to Moffat for their health.

In a small way Moffat then contributed to the woollen industry of the Borders although there was no central mill or factory. The weavers, working in their own homes, made among other things a Moffat tartan which is mentioned in the ballad *Aiken Drum* - 'His plaid was of the Moffat tartan'. In the controversy about the origin of tartans, this bears out the theory that one particular tartan was indigenous to a district rather than to a family or clan.

The opening of the new Glasgow-Carlisle road in 1819-20, which ran through Beattock, up the Evan valley and over the Summit (1029'), deprived Moffat of much of the coaching traffic and seriously affected the hotel business for a time. The Edinburgh mails, however, still went through Moffat on the old road which ascended the steep hill to the Beef Tub by Ericstane Brae. A few years later this road was diverted to its present course, an undertaking which incurred considerable expense. In fact the route was thought to be in such excellent condition after this that the Post Office tightened its regulations and would brook no excuses for delay in mail deliveries.

On the morning of February 8th, 1831, the Edinburgh mail-coach left Dumfries in a blinding snowstorm, reaching Moffat in the early afternoon. It was intensely cold and whirling snow showers still rocketed from a leaden sky. Against the best advice, Goodfellow the driver and McGeorge the guard decided to continue the journey, fearing the consequences of delay. An extra pair of horses was harnessed to the coach and one or two local men who knew the road joined the passengers inside. A mile and a half beyond Moffat the coach stuck fast. One pair of horses carried the men back to the town to fetch a chaise for the two women passengers while the driver and the guard went on with the mails on the other pair. They soon returned, however, having found it impossible to continue on horseback, and Goodfellow urged McGeorge to give up the attempt. But nothing would shake the guard's determination to carry out his duty and the driver refused to desert him so the two men set out on foot with mail bags, weighing seven stone, over their shoulders. Meantime the storm increased in fury and the two women left alone in the coach, fearing they would be snowed under, started to scream for help which fortunately was not long in coming.

The driver and the guard did not return to Moffat that night as everyone expected. Early next day the road contractor, James Marchbanks, set off on a tour of inspection and after plodding through nearly six miles of deep snow, found the mail bags hanging on a snow - post not far from Tweedshaws. The immense drifts made it impossible for him to go on any further and returning to Moffat, he collected a rescue party who, with lanterns and poles, started a wide-spread search for the missing men. Next day they were joined by a larger body of men with spades and pick-axes but their efforts were unsuccessful and it was not until February 12th

The top of the High Street looking towards Academy Street just after the construction of the
Colvin Fountain in 1875

*The Hydropathic just after completion in 1878. The stables are clearly visible in the grounds
of the market garden and the laundry lies to the right of them*

19

that the two dead bodies were found near Tweedshaws Cross. A hundred years later in 1931, a memorial was erected to Goodfellow and McGeorge near this spot.

The curious circumstances of the discovery, related in a letter to the *Moffat Times* in 1899 by William Kirk, son of the Tweedshaws innkeeper, relies for documentary evidence on his testimony. On the 11th February, 1831, Kirk says, his father was visited by the Tweedshaws toll-keeper who told him he had dreamt that he saw Goodfellow walking bare-headed with a shepherd at Tweedshaws Cross. After a moment's hesitation, the innkeeper then described how he had also dreamt of McGeorge in the same place. The two men left the main body of searchers early next morning, and arriving at the spot they had dreamt of, found the frozen bodies under the snow, lying a few yards from each other.

SCHOOLING IN THE TOWN

In 1639 Dr Robert Johnstone, a relative of the Annandale family and brother-in-law to 'Jingling Geordie' Heriot of Edinburgh, left in his Will £1000 for the endowment of a Grammar School in Moffat, 'the teaching staff to consist of a master, with 500 merks (£27.75) of yearly salary; an usher with 200 (£11.11); and a commercial or visiting master with 150 merks - all money of the Realm of Scotland'. The Will entrusted the appointment of teachers to the Town Council and ministers of Edinburgh, the local supervision being put in the hands of 'Lord Johnstone and his heirs and the ministers of Moffat for the time being.' The School was apparently established soon after although there seems to have been some dissatisfaction about the execution of Dr Johnstone's conditions, one complaint being the absence of a commercial master. It was first housed in a building which stood in the middle of the High Street near the site of the present War Memorial but about 1772 this was demolished and the School moved into the newly-built Court House which still stands at the corner of High Street and Well Street.

Under this roof was accommodated the Court House, the Grammar School and the Town Jail, which must surely have been distracting for both pupils and masters on occasion. The history of the Jail, however, seems to have been mild, the last event of any interest being the lodgment there of a party of French prisoners. Escaping from Edinburgh, they had been discovered on a hillside near Granton subisting on the Laird's sheep which they innocently described as "wild moutons".

The reputation of the school suffered in 1699 when a threat to remove one of the pupils resulted in his being flogged to death by the Rector, a man named Robert Carmichael. For this he was tried and convicted at Edinburgh and 'sentenced to be taken through the streets of Edinburgh, and to be given eighteen sharp strokes with a whip by the hangman at three crowded parts of the city and then expelled from the country.'

The schools of the day often touted for business in the local newspapers and journals and the following advertisment, which appeared in *The Dumfries and Galloway Courier* in 1827, describes the educational wares of the school at that time.

BOARD AND EDUCATION AT MOFFAT.

John Beattie, M.A., Rector of the Grammar School and Academy of Moffat, can accomodate a few boarders at 20 gns. each per annum including public and private education in Latin, Greek, arithmetic, English grammar; but French, geography and book-keeping are charged extra. The situation of Moffat is well-known for being very healing, and the Rector's house is detatched from the village upon the road to the mineral waters. To the institution belongs a Rector and two assistants, all under the patronage of the Honourable the Town Council and the reverend clergy of Edinburgh and the heir of the Annandale Estates as trustees. This institution has no connection with the sceeder Academy here, and meets on the first Monday of October. The most respectable references will be given if required.

The 'sceeder' Academy referred to was probably Morison's School in Well Street which at that time counted about a hundred pupils and was 'confined strictly to English education' for 'the children of natives only'. The School was founded in 1839 with £2000 left for this purpose by a Moffat man, William Morison, whose business career in Glasgow, New York, and the East Indies had been remarkably successful. In 1860 there was also a Seminary for Young Ladies in Hopetoun Place, an Infant School in Well Street and an Industrial School at Millburn Bridge. In 1834 the original Grammar School and the Parish School were amalgamated and became the Moffat Academy.

During this century a number of private schools were operated, perhaps the most prominent of which was St Ninian's. Since its recent closure, the school, which can be seen at the top of Well Street, is to be renovated and converted into apartments for retired RAF personnel. This is the most fitting use to which the building could be put since Sir Hugh Dowding was born there in 1882 and as Air Chief Marshal during the Second World War masterminded victory during the Battle of Britain. A memorial to him stands in the Station Park, over which a lone Spitfire flies each Rememberance Sunday.

THE BARDS

Robert Burns visited Moffat on several occasions, probably on account of his friendship with Mr James Clarke, the school-master and librarian, who left the district in 1794 for not 'sorting with' the Moffatonians as Burns describes it in a letter. The poet was inspired to scratch his well-known *Apology for a Scrimpit Nature* on a window-pane at the Black Bull one day after Miss Deborah Davies, the petite English Beauty, had ridden past with a friend of more generous proportions.

The main entrance to the Hydropathic at the rear of the building, 1878. Sulphur water was piped to the Hydro from the Moffat Well over the Gallows Hill behind

The inner hall of the Hydro prior to its complete destruction in 1921 when the building was gutted by fire

Ask why God made the gem so small,
An' why so huge the granite?
Because God meant mankind should set
The higher value on it.

The words are still printed above the window, although the original pane of glass has disappeared, some believe to Russia. To this minute siren, he also wrote the songs *Lovely Davies* and *The Bonnie Wee Thing*.

Burns is also said to have 'roamed the woods of Dumcrieff and Craigieburn' (one mile out from Moffat on the Selkirk road, by Moffat Water) and to have composed some of his lyrics there. He must certainly have known Craigieburn where lived the fascinating Jean Lorimer with whom Burns interceded on account of a friend. To her he wrote many of his best lyrics, including *Craigieburn Wood*.

Sweet fa's the eve on Craigieburn
And blythe awakes the morrow;
But a' the pride o' Spring's return
Can yield me nought but sorrow.

I see the flowers and spreading trees,
I hear the wild birds singing;
But what a weary wight can please,
And care his bosom ringing?

Fain, fain, would I my griefs impart
Yet daurna for your anger;
But secret love will break my heart,
If I conceal it langer.

If thou refuse to pity me;
If thou shalt love anither,
When yon green leaves fade frae the trees,
Around my grave they'll wither.

Although Burns was courting by proxy for a fellow exciseman named Gillespie, the love songs held such passionate appeal that they 'occasioned much scandalous talk' in Dumfries. After the publication of *Craigieburn Wood*, Burns wrote to his publishers 'the young lady on whom it was made is one of the finest women in Scotland, and in fact, *entre nous*, is, in a manner to me what Sterne's Eliza was to him, a mistress, friend or what you will, in the guileless simplicity of Platonic love.'

But in spite of Burns' efforts, the unhappy Gillespie was rejected and soon after Jean eloped with a young farmer from Barnhill who was also madly in love with her. Driving back from an evening party at Poldean, it is said that instead of leaving her at Craigieburn, he drove furiously to Gretna Green. Whether this was against her will or not, she soon had reason to repent it for her husband drank and gambled his way to Carlisle prison, leaving Jean to fend for herself. Many years afterwards, broken in health, alone and penniless in Edinburgh, she was offered the post of housekeeper to an old gentlemen who had been told she was once an inspiration to Burns.

In more jovial mood Burns wrote the ballad *Willie brewed a peck o' maut* not far from Craigieburn on the site where Burns Cottage (Waterside) now stands. 'The air is Masterson's, the song mine', Burns wrote, 'The occasion of it was this: Mr William Nicol of the High School, Edinburgh, during the Autumn vacation, being at Moffat, honest Allan, who was at that time on a visit to Dalswinton, and I went to pay Nicol a visit. We had such a joyous meeting that Mr Masterson and I agreed, each in our own way, that we should celebrate the business'.

Sir Walter Scott, too, must have known Moffat although it is seldom mentioned in his own writing or in his numerous biographies. James Hogg, the Ettrick Shepherd, however, describes a visit to Loch Skene and Moffat with Scott, Willie Laidlaw, the Abbotsford factor, and Sir Adam Ferguson.

I conducted them through that wild region, by a path which, if not rode by Clavers, was I dare say, never rode by another gentlemen. Sir Adam rode into a gulph inadvertently and got a sad fright, but Scott, in the very worst paths, never dismounted, save at Loch Skene to take some dinner. We went to Moffat that night, where we met with some of his family, and such a day and night of glee I never witnessed. Our perils were matter to him of infinite merriment; and there was a short-tempered boot boy at the inn who wanted to pick a quarrel with him, at which he laughed till the water ran over his cheeks. I was disappointed in never seeing some incident in his subsequent works laid in a scene resembling the rugged solitudes around Loch Skene, for I never saw him survey any scene with so much attention. A single serious look at the scene generally filled his mind with it, and he seldom took another; but here he took all the names of all the hills and their altitudes and relative situations with regard to one another and made me repeat them several times.

In a note at the end of *The Heart of Midlothian*, Scott describes the original of Madge Wildfire as a wandering shepherdess called Feckless Fanny who drove a small flock of sheep about the countryside.

She had for each a different name, to which it answered when it was called by its mistress, and would likewise obey in the most suprising manner any command she thought proper to give. . . . When she lay down in the fields at night, for she would never enter a house, they always disputed who should lie next to her, by which means she was kept warm, while she lay in the midst of them; when she attempted to rise from the ground, an old ram, whose name was Charlie, always claimed the sole right of assisting her; pushing any that stood in his way aside, until he arrived right before his mistress; he then bowed his head nearly to the ground so that she might lay her hands on his horns, which were very large; he then raised her gently from

A four-in-hand about to start out for St Mary's Loch from the Hydro in the early years of this century. Outings of this nature were a common attraction for visitors to Moffat

The Moffat Well, c 1877, discovered by Rachel Whiteford in 1633 who chanced upon it when out walking one day. The brick-built rear portion still exists

the ground by raising his head. If she chanced to leave her flock feeding, as soon as they discovered she had gone, they all began to bleat most piteously, and would continue to do so till she returned; they would then testify their joy by rubbing their sides against her petticoat, and frisking about.

Passing through Moffat one day, Charlie broke into a kailyard and was hunted to death by the owner's mastiff. This nearly broke Feckless Fanny's heart and 'she would not part from the side of her old friend for several days, and it was with much difficulty that she consented to allow him to be buried.' The old ram's grave, which she visited every year, was called 'The Leddy's Knowe' and Scott maintains that the Moffat schoolboys 'held it sacred' in his day. Scott vouches for the truth of the tale but whether Ladyknowe is the site of Charlie's grave or not is open to conjecture.

THE WATERS

Moffat Well, sulphurous source of so much of the town's later prosperity and importance, was discovered in 1633 by Bishop Whiteford's daughter who married a Johnstone of Corehead and settled in the district. That a fine lady of the 17th Century should make such a discovery is less curious than it seems for she was apparently in the habit of visiting Spas and immediately recognised the taste and smell of the healing waters which have been described as 'resembling bilge water or the scourings of a foul gun'. It was not for sometime, however, that Moffat became the fashionable Spa which later attracted so many visitors from all over Great Britain in search of health and gaiety. During the 18th and 19th Centuries numbers of booklets and treatise were published analysing the mineral waters and extolling the fresh air of Moffat. 'The climate of Moffat,' records one of these, 'is said to be so remarkably healthy as to occasion sneezing and other marks of oxygenation in persons not accustomed to it'.

By 1745 the description of early morning scenes at the Well seem to establish Moffat as a favourite watering-place. 'Morning is the approved time of visiting the Well,' runs one account, 'and on fine mornings a visitor or two may be forward by six o'clock; but it is not till about seven that there is any decided evidence of briskness. Pedestrians then begin to stream in, and about half an hour later two or three omnibuses, and sometimes several other vehicles, add their contents to the swelling tide, and the verandah is completely animated; the company present - ladies, gentlemen and children - numbering perhaps two hundred. It is the bounden duty of one and all to drink.'

John Home was not complimentary about the site of the unsheltered Well but left his explanation of its popularity in the following four lines.

No grace did nature here bestow;
But wise was Nature's aim:
She bade the healing waters flow,
And straight the graces came.

Nevertheless, there were many serious Well-drinkers who even went to the length of hiring 'conveniences for bathing' in the waters. These were deep wooden tubs which were kept by an old woman and 'lent out for a trifle'. The water was brought down from the Well by an old man in carts and sold for so much a barrel. The bather then 'popped into his tub, and drew a cloth about his neck to confine the steam'.

The Industrial Revolution put an end to the weavers' trade in Moffat but the place grew in importance as a sheep farming centre and continued to flourish as a Spa. In fact in 1859 the gaiety and enthusiasm of the Well-drinkers knew no bounds, the first assembly of the day gathering between half-past seven and eight o'clock in the morning. 'On a fine morning the walk is very picturesque and enjoyable', one visitor wrote, 'and a Band of Music is stationed at the Well to assist the drinking - three large tumblers being the statutory quantum. As several hundred usually assemble at this time, the Well is not a little gay and the walk there and back does much to appetize the visitors for breakfast - the lazy, infirm or junenile having, however, the facility of riding in a bus'. The waters of Hartfell mineral spring (Chalybeate), discovered in 1748 while excavations for copper ore were in progress, were even bottled and exported as far as India, as well as to nearer destinations. This source corresponds to the legendary Fountain of Galabes, where Merlin spent the last years of his life in the late sixth century.

The Baths Hall, 'comprising assembly hall and reading rooms, with suites of bathing apartments behind,' was built in 1827 in the classical style so popular at the time. Here 'Promenade Concerts', Assembly Balls, picture exhibitions and all manner of entertainments took place, the reading room being the news distribution centre before penny newspapers came in. *The Moffat Register and Annandale Observer* describes one of these balls in glowing colours.

THE GRAND SEPTEMBER BALL

This fete which has been turning the heads of a few debutantes, and been wearisomely engaging the fingers of many needlewomen for months, came at last and eclipsed every conception. So sudden was the wizardry of transition accomplished that the 'show', which up till four o'clock had occupied the place continuously with passing crowds, was completely removed, the whole place cleaned, re-adorned and re-set and by eight o'clock was already booming with the lustre of beauty, and was dazzling and blazing in silk, poplin, muslin, gauze, laces, jewellery, bouquets, fans, 'silken shoon' , fairy feet, starry eyes, smiles, white vests, swallow-tails, unmentionables, slippers and clustering locks of various hues. Small talk, jokes, confabulation, confidential whispers and pouting complaints filled the air; while the eye was all a-tremble with the glare, glitter, and garishness of tint, texture and toilette. Music - the poetry of sound - and dancing - the poetry of motion - took all of a sudden the vows of marriage and the wedded 'mythi' speedily set their votaries to the pleasing task. . . .

Reporters in those days, while paying scant attention to punctuation and grammar, must surely have carried about with them a text book of adjectives.

Moffat also saw the gaunt, forbidding figure of Thomas Carlyle from time to time. The frivolities of Assembly Balls and Spa-drinking were not for him. As a poor student he tramped the long road from his home in Ecclefechan to Edinburgh and this took him through Moffat and over the Beef Tub, but in his later famous days, he still strode silently about the countryside looking more like a tramp than a celebrated philosopher. A well-known lady in Moffat, mistaking him for a beggar resting by the roadside, once offered him twopence out of the kindness of her heart. He was not popular in his home town. Froude, his biographer, arriving at Ecclefechan for the great man's funeral, remarked to the station-master that he hoped there would be no disorderly crush. "Never fear, sir", was the reply, "there's no an auld wife in 'Fechan wad come tae see him living, an' they'll no trouble theirsels noo he's deid".

In the last half of the 19th Century Moffat made rapid strides in civic progress and became a flourishing residential place. The Gas Company was formed in 1837 when 'shop and parlour in the course of the Autumn were in the brilliant enjoyment of gas-light.' The opening of the Caledonian Railway line between Beattock and Carlisle in 1847 and on to Dumfries and Edinburgh the following year, brought visitors who 'long in city pent', now came not only for the season but all the year round whenever they could get away from business. In 1864 Moffat became a Burgh under the General Police and Improvements Act and before the end of the century, four churches and a vast hydropathic had been built, besides a number of good-sized houses in and around the town.

The establishment of the Hydro, overlooking the Annan Water in April 1878, finally afforded Moffat the type of facilities which had been long-overdue. It rapidly enhanced Moffat's reputation as a Spa second only to Harrogate, but the Hydro's mock neo-Gothic style and Victorian atmosphere dissapeared in a blaze of fire when it was gutted in 1921. Since the First World War it had been in a decline compounded by the depression and the influence of the motor car and there is some rumour as to how the blaze started.

Many towns blessed with such a facility might have felt the loss to a greater degree, but, to the town's credit little else has changed. The broad extent of its thoroughfares and streets are still apparent and, even now, it is still possible to take the picturesque walks to both of the Wells on which the town's prosperity was established. Recently, both the Hartfell and the Sulphurous springs have been renovated to a degree which now allows any casual visitor to go and visit them. The longer walk to the former is perhaps the more rewarding since the water is both palatable and refreshing after the two and a half mile climb from the Annan Water. And although the pungent water at the latter is an acquired taste it is not inconceivable that visitors will again be seen ambling up the Well Road at dawn to 'take the waters'.